LANDMARK COLLECTOR'S LIBRARY

ECHOES
THE DALES

Events, People & Places in the 1950s
in & around Matlock, Derbyshire

Ron Duggins

Page 1: The final Matlock Open tennis tournament was held in 1953. Over the years the event, organised by the town's attractions committee on the Hall Leys Park, had attracted entries from all over the world and seen here is Miss J Attwood from New Zealand receiving the C Walter Evans Rose Bowl from the Duke of Devonshire.

Opposite page: Members of Matlock and District Amateur Swimming Club proudly show off their trophies at the Lido. Barry Spencer (440 yards champion), Pauline Askew (junior girls champion), Rose McCann (ladies club champion) and Alan Andrews (junior diving champion) are pictured with Barry Kay, John Hopkinson, Nigel Bryant, June and Janet Smith, Bridget Wilson, Brian Evans, Susan Lea and Jean Askew.

LANDMARK COLLECTOR'S LIBRARY

ECHOES OF THE DALES

Events, People & Places in the 1950s
in & around Matlock, Derbyshire

Ron Duggins

Landmark Publishing

Published by

Ashbourne Hall, Cokayne Ave
Ashbourne, Derbyshire DE6 1EJ England
Tel: (01335) 347349 Fax: (01335) 347303
e-mail: landmark@clara.net
web site: www.landmarkpublishing.co.uk

ISBN 13: 978-1-84306-306-3

ISBN 10: 1-84306-306-9

British Library Cataloguing in Publication Data: a catalogue
record for this book is available from the British Library.

Printed by Cromwell Press Ltd, Trowbridge

Front cover: The highlight of the Matlock Carnival festivity in 1954 was the swimming gala in
the town's open-air pool. Crowds here are watching a mop fight while Malcolm Sellers and Alan
Andrews hold the platform.

Back cover top: Petallers working on the "The Holy Bible" tableau,
for the 1954 Wirksworth well dressing festival.

Back cover middle: The Scouts and Brownies annual Rally of 1952 on the Cromford Meadows. This
picture shows the gymnastic display led by Mick Slater (centre), and including Peter Jones, Gordon
Statham and Neil Jury.

Back cover bottom: A fancy dress parade in 1954 organised by Darley Dale County Primary
School. Among the entrants on the front row are first prize winners Ian Hodgkinson as
Hiawatha, Sandra Hodgkinson in her Easter bonnet, and Ann Milton as Drummer Dyes.

Contents

Dedication

All towns, villages and districts have their characters, some more "notorious" than others, but all held with a kind of fondness. In the Matlock area were two who left a greater legacy than they could ever have believed possible. They were Ella Smith and Harry Gill. Ella (often referred to as Red Ella because of her political leanings) was founder and editor in the 1930s of Coming Events, a free sheet which she later re-named the Matlock Mercury and West Derbyshire News. Harry (often referred to as Hoppy, due to his pronounced limp) was the district's photographer and over the years he serviced the Mercury and other newspapers with pictures from most "happenings" that took place. Many of his pictures and negatives were destroyed, but most of those in this book were taken by him and have been saved by me for posterity. My association with the pair began in 1951 when I joined the staff of Smith's Printing Works, which was owned by Herbert Smith, Ella's husband. At that time the Mercury was a small operation, slotted in between the jobbing printing which was being carried out at the Bakewell Road premises. Eventually the Mercury expanded, jobbing printing ceased, and the newspaper began its full-time coverage of life as it happened in the district. That life is now reflected in this book.

This photograph of Mrs Smith was taken from the Riber Castle grounds and shows Matlock below.

Harry Gill is photographed outside his shop and darkroom in Matlock Bath.

Ambergate

Winners of the DFA Medals competition in 1955 were the Ambergate Football Club. They beat Darley Dale United by two goals to nil on the Causeway Lane Ground in Matlock – both goals being scored by Taylor. The Ambergate team pictured with their medals is Radford, Byard, Davenport, Coupe, Dakin, Sully, Flint, Mason C, Mason H, and Flinders.

Beeley

Beeley village's memento of the Queen's Coronation was the unveiling of a seat in 1954. The ceremony was performed on the village green under the Prince of Wales' Tree by Mrs Mary Hutchinson, the oldest female resident in Beeley. Watching her are (left to right) Ann Towndrow, Michael Marsden, Stuart Rutherford, Heather Gilbert, Herbert Parker, Doris Parker, Raymond Jeffreys and Mr Leslie Cantrill.

Pretty Sandra Critchlow was crowned as Beeley's first carnival queen in 1952. She was crowned by Mrs Hargreaves, of Darley Dale, and her attendants were Pamela Mayfield, Doris Parker, Janet Holmes and Shelagh Marsden. After a service in the church which was conducted by Canon S E Longland, the royalty were processed through the village in a horse drawn carriage.

Beeley 'Carnival Royalty' in a rural setting outside the village hall in 1953. Left to right (back row) Doris Parker, Barbara Bond, Pamela Mayfield, Sandra Critchlow, 'Queen' Beverley Allsop, Gwen Fearn, Heather Gilbert and Joy Hammersley; (front) Janet Holmes, Geoffrey Fearn and Shirley Marsden.

Dull skies failed to dampen the spirit of Beeley carnival in June 1958 when the crowning ceremony was transferred into the Duke's Barn. Queen Shelagh Marsden (13) was crowned by Mrs Wilkes before a large crowd, and her attendants were Heather Gilbert, Joy Hammersley, Judith Critchlow and Marlene Gilbert. Page-boy was Malcolm Gilbert.

May Day celebrations were always a happy occasion at Beeley School and 1955 was no exception. Scholars at the school chose Janet Holmes as their Queen and she was duly crowned with flowers and a daisy chain. Headmistress Mrs G A Storer and her assistant Miss J Hutchinson are pictured with Janet and her retinue which included Marlene Gilbert, Gloria Wigley (petal strewers), Roy Hammersley, John Hancock (pages), Anne Towndrow (maid of honour), Frank Robinson (escort), John Grindey (daisy chain bearer), Sheila Cantrill (crown bearer), David Jeffery (ring bearer) and Lavinia Towndrow (posy bearer).

Bonsall

The best season for thirty years was how Bonsall Football Club president Mr T H Poundall described their performance during the 1953-54 season. The last time a trophy came to the village was in 1924 when chairman Mr Frank Land was in the team – and his son Gerald was in the present one. The club were runners-up in the Horace Holmes Cup, the Trustees Shield and the Rowsley and District League championship but they won the High Peak Cup which Mr Poundall is seen presenting to captain Henry Rickards. Also in the picture is Herbert Loxley who was captain of the team three years previously when they won DFA medals and who became the first Bonsall player to play professional football – for Notts County. Also in the group are Alf Bunting, Teddy Thorneycroft, Dennis Bond, Geoff Buckley, Terry Barrett, Freddy Roose, Eric Massey, Frank Land, Gerald Land, Doxey, Hoult and Pugh.

Bonsall Boys Endowed School football team who played during the 1949-50 season are pictured with their teacher Mr Alistair Storey. They are left to right (back row) Paddy Holland, Henry Rickards, Brian Hobson, Ronnie Loxley, and Ivan Spencer, (front row) Darrell Buckley, Terence Baker, George Fearn, Eric Massey, Adrian Cordin, Matthew Flint and Gerald Land.

Football played a great part in the lives of boys at Bonsall Endowed School. Winners of the South Peak Schools League 2 championship they are left to right (back row) Darrell Buckley, Norman Bond, Ian Spencer, Matthew Flint, Adrian Cordin, Boden and Dennis Bond, (front row) Peter Gratton, Pugh, Henry Rickards, Gerald Land, Joe Walker and ball-boy Arthur Bond.

If Bonsall Football Club were to be congratulated on their 1953-54 season no-one could have foreseen the following season. Winners of the Rowsley League championship, the Horace Holmes Cup, and Trustees Shield, they were only beaten in the final of the DFA Medals by Manchester United's "nursery" team High Lees. Played at Whaley Bridge, four bus loads of supporters saw them go down by 2-1. Herbert Loxley – Bonsall's Notts County player – was guest of honour at the club dinner when he presented the trophies to captain Henry Rickards. Others pictured include Jimmy Timms, Tom Latham, Teddy Thorneycroft, Frank Land, Adrian Cordin, Peter Hawley, Doxey, Alf Bunting, Geoff Buckley and Hoult.

As well as football, Bonsall has another claim to fame…well dressings. First prize in 1954 went to "The Saviour and Nicodemus" dressed by Messrs Poundall, Austin and Wild, while the junior well winners were Janice and Anita Austin with "The Good Shepherd". Pictured with their wells are Tom and Ada Poundall and Tom Austin, and Janice Austin, Movita Gratton, Alice Bunting and Joan Knighton.

There was cause for a double celebration in the Wild household during Bonsall Well Dressings Festival and Carnival in August 1958. Winnie Wild (19) was crowned carnival queen on the opening day of the week-long festivities and the following week the well she designed took first prize. She is pictured by the well, "The Ten Lepers", with her mother and Miss Sheila Alesbrook.

A call for a memorial to honour the memory of Alderman Charles White, former chairman of Derbyshire County Council and a native of Bonsall, was made by Mr Herbert Hardy when he opened the village's annual horticultural show. Mr Hardy, himself a former Bonsall resident, described Mr White as "One of the greatest men Derbyshire has ever produced." Left to right are Mr S Ollerenshaw (judge), Mr Hardy, Miss W Jackson (judge), Mr A Millward (judge) and Councillor Sam Elliott (president).

Crich

Crich Boys Football Club were champions of the Rowsley and District Youth League in the 1950-51 season and celebrated their success with a social evening in the Parish Room. Secretary Don Nadin made the arrangements and tea was served by the ladies committee. The North Western Road Car Co. Sports & Social Club donated the trophy and medals, that were presented by its chairman, Mr Geoff Birkett, of Matlock. Pictured outside the Bull's Head at Crich with Mr Birkett are (left to right) Colin Harrison, Arthur Fox, Harry Williamson, Derek Swindell (captain), Bernard Booth, Derek Taylor, Jackie McCann, Alan Dakin, Terry Wainwright and Aubrey Briddon. Bernard's father, Cyril, was licensee of the Bull's Head where the teams changed before the long walk to the pitch in the big meadow on the way to Plaistow Green. Several members recall that long walk in winter and how quickly their studs wore out on the tarmac road.

Matlock Young Farmers' annual ploughing match and show was held at Wakebridge Farm, Crich, in 1953 where the quality and quantity of exhibits was extremely high. The day was hosted by Thomas Walker and his family who had earlier bought the farm which was part of an early monastery. Before moving there Mr Walker had carried on the family high-class butchery business in Holloway and which had been in their possession for 100 years.

Cromford

Elected in July as Cromford carnival queen for 1952 was Miss Margaret Else, of The Hill. She is seen flanked by her attendants Shirley Brooks (left) and Hilda Baker (right). Margaret was 16 years old, Shirley 16 and Hilda 21. Judges were Mrs Winifred Dimmock, Miss G Allen and Mr Peter Carley, with Martin Beresford as MC.

Grey skies followed by sunshine were a feature at the opening of Cromford and Scarthin Wakes Carnival in September 1954 when Mrs Berrill, wife of Wirksworth Dr F R Berrill crowned 16-year-old Janet Batterley as Queen. Pictured after the ceremony on the top photograph are Joan Lucas, Doris Hallows, Mrs Berrill, Queen Janet, "Miss Cromford" Joyce Walker, Mary Fern, Pearl Osborne, Susan Charlesworth, Stanley Kniveton and Enid Hinchcliffe. Festivies continued on Monday night with a carnival procession up Cromford Hill into North Street where the judging of fancy dress and decorated vehicles took place.

The final carnival of the district was always Cromford's in September and at the 1955 event chairman Cyril Kidd celebrated 25 years service to the organisation. Funds raised went to charities and particularly the Cromford Old Age Pensioners Association. Queen of the festivities was Kathleen Webster and her attendants were Dorothy Shooter, Eunice Hilton, Norma Vallance and Pauline Webster. Kathleen was crowned by Mrs F Jones, of Ashbourne, who is pictured with 1954 Queen Janet Batterley and her attendants Doris Hallows, Mary Fearn, Enid Hinchliffe and Susan Charlesworth. Also on the picture are Robert Graham, Cyril Kidd, Charles Widdeson and George Batterley. Monday was always fancy dress parade night when crowds lined the streets. Regular entrant was Joey Robinson as Charlie Chaplin with his urchin friend Martin Johnston (pictured on page 17) and they were joined by dozens of others, some of whom are pictured and include Daylene Potter (Swedish Flower Girl), Brian Skinner (Space Commander), Linda Notley (Summer Time), Raymond Williams (Boys of the Old Brigade) and Suasan Smith (Little Bo Peep). A touch of the Scottish Highlands was supplied by Cromford Garnetters in the decorated lorry section.

Fine weather helped to swell the coffers of Cromford Carnival committee's charity chest, with £180 being collected during the festivities in September 1958. Mrs Bernard Swain crowned Miss Anne Clewes Carnival Queen and her attendants were Mary Byrne and Anne Moore while junior attendants were Judy Bond and Susan Wain. Miss Jennifer Inckle (retiring queen) was invested as Miss Cromford, and was attended by Maureen Turner, Ann Darvill, Janet Allsop and Patricia Goodhead.

The Duke of Devonshire (left) was on hand to present the prizes in a Derbyshire Round of "The People" national darts championships in 1951 at the Bell Inn, Cromford. Among those pictured are John Land, Jack Turner (referee), Herbert Rickards and Mr Holt.

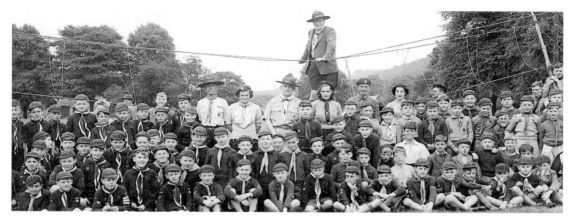

Scouts, Brownies and leaders from all over the district massed on Cromford Meadows for their annual Rally in 1952. Demonstrations included tent rigging, a signalling tower, an aerial ropeway and a monkey bridge. Assistant County Commissioner Harold Fletcher, District Commissioner W H Briggs and Miss Barbara Haslam are pictured with some of those who took part. One of the highlights was a gymnastic display led by Mick Slater (centre), and including Peter Jones, Gordon Statham and Neil Jury.

Darley Dale

Above: In 1951 two Darley Dale footballers were chosen to play for Derbyshire Boys against Cheshire Boys. Maurice Watts (left) and Raymond Grindey (right) also played for the South Peak Schools XI and Hackney Foresters in the Rowsley and District Youth League. Centre forward Watts later signed for Notts County and Aston Villa before his career was interrupted by National Service. On demob he played for Matlock Town where he scored a hat-trick on his debut. Centre half Grindey signed amateur forms with Blackpool.

Left: July 1955 saw 21-year old Keith Marsden of Darley Dale transferred from Chesterfield FC to Manchester City for £8,000. Centre-forward Keith scored four goals in five matches for Chesterfield while on leave from the Royal Air Force.

Darley Dale FC won the Hope Valley League for the second successive year in 1953 and also won the Elton Cup both of which are on display along with the players who formed the 1st and 2nd teams. Left to right (standing) Len Evans (secretary), Pete Moran, Wilf Ridge (referee), Harry Siddall, Raymond Grindley, Arthur Vardy (committee member), Eric Wright, Ron Rowland, Cyril Hickman (committe member), Rupert Wood, Roy Boden, George Holloway, Graham Brookhouse (2nd team captain), Bernard Cooper, reg Humphreys (trainer), Brian Boam, Reg Smith, Fred Bond (chairman), Ernie Walker, Fred Walker (treasurer); (kneeling) George Briddon (committee member), Ken Grafton, Stan Wood, Gene Woodhouse, Clarence Askew (1st team captain), Rex Fulloway, Maurice Watts, Ron Cope, Bernard Oldfield, Paddy Lambe (committee member)

A 6-0 drubbing of Wessington United gave Darley United the Matlock and District League Junior Cup in a match that was held over from the previous season. Captain Clarence Askew received the Cup from Mr Cyril Harrison watched by team-mates Frank Middleton, Ken Grafton, Geoff Marsh, Gene Woodhouse, Eric Wright and Brian Boam. Aubrey Evans, the 6-year-old son of club secretary Len is in the foreground.

Winners of the singles and doubles titles in the 1954 South Peak tennis championships at the Whitworth Institute, Darley Dale, were Mrs E Walker, Charles Dunne, Hans Espig, Olive Peacock, Ken Black, Mrs J Hescroft, Alan Towndrow and Mrs Mary Cope.

For the third successive year Matlock All Saints' School beat Darley Dale County Primary in the local schools quiz. Questions ranging from spelling, natural history and geography to general knowledge were set by students from Matlock Training College and the final scores were All Saints 116 points Darley Dale 85. Members of the two teams were (left to right, back row) Stuart Turner, Peter Espig, David Wright, John Kersey, Graham Jepson, Alan Wright, Malcolm Taylor and David Taylor; (front row) Rhona Hallows, Susan Wright, Barbara Lewis, Wendy Peck, Patricia Jolley, Jacqueline Bowler, Jacqueline Taylor and Eileen Briddon.

The increasing difficulty in finding suitable jobs for school-leavers was likely to get worse warned Headmaster Mr Joe Hancock at Darley Dale Secondary School's second speech day in 1954, urging parents to consider allowing their children to stay on even after the normal leaving age. Prize and trophy winners here include Barry Hill, Sylvia Wilson, Patricia Morton, Albert Hopkinson, John Pope, Brian Else, Donald Macdonald, Thelma Ball, and Malcolm Sellers.

These members of the Oker Tree Players had plenty to smile about in December 1953 when they performed "Winning Smiles" – a football pools comedy. Pictured in South Darley Village Hall they are, left to right (standing) Eddie Kean, Gerald West, Hilda Gilbert, and Derek Booth; (seated) Joan Simcock, Maud Allen, Tom Simcock, Mary Wright and Joan Porter.

As the year drew to its close, pupils of Darley Dale County Primary School put on their annual concert. Pictured are some of those who took part in the colourful spectacle, including David Horobin, Roy Stevenson, Michael Fletcher, David Taylor, Jackie Bowler, Susan Lea, Patricia Lomas, Michael Knowles, Margaret Cass, Heather Taylor, Ivan Hardy, Eric Gascoigne and Graham Jepson.

A fancy dress parade in 1954 organised by Darley Dale County Primary School attracted a good entry in the Whitworth Intitute when judges were Mr and Mrs J S Wain and Mrs Ella Smith. Among the entrants on the front row are first prize winners Ian Hodgkinson as Hiawatha, Sandra Hodgkinson in her Easter bonnet, and Ann Milton as Drummer Dyes.

Thirty couples who had been married at St Mary's Church, South Darley, went back there in 1952 to a special service of remembrance. Oldest couple present were Mr and Mrs Sam Edge, of The Yews, Oaker, where they had lived all their married life and where Mrs Edge as Mary Marsden was born. Also present were Mr and Mrs James Bark, of Oaker Road, and their daughter Zoe and her husband Godfrey. Mr and Mrs Bark were married in 1924 and their daughter in 1951. The Rev I O Evans conducted the service after which the couples had tea and entertainment in Cross Green School.

Popular police constable Len Lea said his farewells in 1958 to the residents of Darley Dale, where he had spent the previous eight years, before moving to Alvaston. Keen sportsman Len played in the county police cricket and tennis teams as well as organising the annual police ball in his role as Divisional Sports club secretary. During the 1939–45 war he served in the Royal Navy, mainly in the Far East. PC and Mrs Lea's daughter Susan won many trophies as a swimming champion.

Proudly showing off their new uniforms for the first time Darley Dale Band played at a Red Cross rally in Whitworth Institute park. The uniforms cost £250 and were paid for by playing at various engagements and by generous help from the ladies' committee. The band was formed in Wensley at the turn of the 19th century and later they moved to South Darley. The band folded in the mid-1960s, the instruments and sheet music sold and an era ended. That is until 1984 when local businessman Dick Marriott helped re-build the Band and Roger Jepson took over the baton in 1988. Pictured at the Red Cross Rally in 1955 are Brian Byard, Michael Marsden, Keith Sheldon, Gordon Hopkinson, Brian Ellis, Jack Boden, Gilroy Stephenson, Ian Garritty and Frank Boylin. Murray Slater, Harold Birkett, Trevor Boam, Arthur Marsden, David Baugh, Dyson Charlesworth and Lewis Charlesworth. Jack Waterfall, Fred Allison, Cyril Sheldon, Douglas Shaw, Jim Garritty, Ernest Boylin, Rex Marsden, Jim Goodwin and Sid Hallows.

Darley Dale Homing Society's annual dinner and prize presentation was held at Ye Olde Englishe Hotel in Matlock when vice-president Sam Wardman was guest of honour. He is pictured (centre seated) with club members who included Mr and Mrs Herbert Duggins and Adrian, Mr and Mrs Jack May, Mr and Mrs Denis Gregory, Mr and Mrs Wilburn Boam and Barry, Mr George Wall, Mr Len Evans, Malcolm Boden and Mr and Mrs Dennis Lane.

H J Enthoven and Sons annual party was held at the New Bath Hotel early in 1955 when guests were joined by the company's medical officer Dr G L Meachim and his wife (extreme right, second row). Others pictured include Ron Broome, Jean Emmerson, Joyce Wilmot, Harry Daniel, Mrs Taylor (wife of Manager Leonard Taylor who was absent through illness), Edith Dakin, Pat Wright, Charles Hollingworth, Willy Lander and Miss Olive Peach, the event organiser.

Part of Darley Dale arrived into the twentieth century in 1955 with the opening of a fully automatic telephone exchange. Originally the area was served manually from Two Dales sub-post office and by 1912 there were 12 subscribers. By 1932 it had moved to a private house on Warney Road with 79 subscribers and from there it was housed in a long wooden shed at the junction of Warney Road and Dale Road with 240 lines. The new £25,000 exchange, on land near Broad Walk, was officially "switched on" by Councillor John Turner who said the service would improve the area's telephone system, already his action had switched 330 subscribers on to an automatic dialling system. The exchange would cater for 500 subscribers but its capacity was 1000 which would cater for the area needs until 1960. Left to right: Councillor Turner, Mr Harold Manton (Telephone Engineers Dept.), Colonel A T J Beard (Nottingham Area Telephone Manager), Mr W T Gemmell (Midland Director, GPO) and Mr Stanley Heathcote (Assistant Telephones Engineer, Matlock District).

Darley Dale's first carnival after the war was held in 1952 when Miss Marian White (15) was crowned queen by Mrs J S Wain, of The Holt, Two Dales. Her attendants were Miss Hilary Bowler and Miss Mavis Fearn, Adrian Charlesworth was page boy. Over 600 people watched the ceremony which took place on the terrace at the Whitworth Institute. The proceedings then moved to the football field where a ladies match was held. Darley Dale Band played selections of music throughout the afternoon – the carnival was revived by the band to raise money for new instruments. Pictured with the queen, her retinue and Mrs Wain are; George Gilberthorpe, A G Groome, Alf Hanson, Mr Wain (Band president), Harold Gill, W Webster, Caroline Smith and Bandsmen Dyson Charlesworth, Jim Garrity, Jack Boden and Fred Allison (secretary).

At a dance in the Whitworth Institute, Derby County goalkeeper, Ray Middleton was one of the judges who chose Marian as Darley Carnival Queen. Her attendants are on her right along with some of the 55 entrants who included Joyce Mellor, Margaret Barrett, Denise McDowell, Betty Pearson and Barbara Watts.

Fancy dress prize winners at the 1952 carnival included Rodney Woodhouse, Adrian Charlesworth, Roy Turkington, Jeffrey Pinkney, Barbara Watts, Caroline Smith, David Champion, Danny McDonald, Sandra Hodgkinson, Carl Woosnam and Ivan Redfern.

Mrs Lalage Wakefield, wife of West Derbyshire MP Mr E B Wakefield crowned South Darley Rose Queen Daphne Wragg in the grounds of Eversleigh House in 1952. Mr Wakefield said what a pleasure it was to leave behind for a short while the politics of Westminster for 'this rural' setting, adding that next year he would have the pleasure of seeing another Queen crowned but his mind always would go back to this simple ceremony. Pictured with Daphne and Mrs and Mr Wakefield are senior attendants Isabel Winthrope and Patricia Haynes, junior maids Doreen Chandler and Janet Haynes, John Pritty and flower girls Susan Woodhouse and Rita Masters along with the Rev I O Evans.

Lea

"Time" was finally called at a Lea public house in 1955 when its licence was withdrawn on the grounds of "redundancy". Landlord for the past 20 years, Arthur Hinds and his wife received farewell gifts of a tankard and brooch from oldest customer Tom Yeomans. Also pictured are Mrs Barbara Fox and Sam Ludlam.

Matlock

A Scented Garden for the Blind was opened in 1955. Funded and provided by the Rotary Club of Matlock it was sited down Olde Englishe Road near to the footbridge over the river. Mrs Gill Orme, one of the organisers of the weekly socials for the Blind officiated at the opening ceremony, accompanied by Rotary president Norman Goward, Rotarian James Woolliscroft and Mrs Woolliscroft, Councillor Remo Tinti and Mr and Mrs Percy Ayre. The garden was created to commemorate the 50th anniversary of Rotary International.

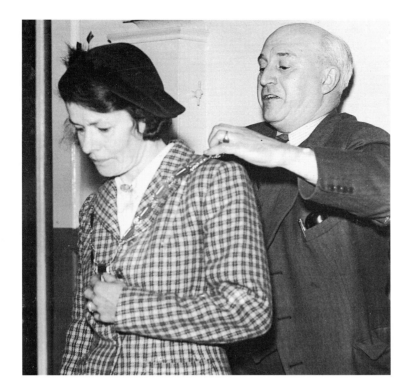

Matlock Urban District Council elected its first-ever woman chairman in 1951. She was Councillor Mrs May Greatorex, who is here seen being invested with her chain of office by outgoing chairman Councillor Frank Rhodes (1949-51).

No-one was seriously injured when this nine-ton lorry careered through the window of the Derwent Valley Co-operative Society shop in Matlock. A shop assistant was cut by flying glass, a woman who was looking in the window received a cut hand and the driver, who jumped clear just before the crash, sustained a cut chin and bruises. The lorry was travelling down Steep Turnpike when the driver appeared to lose control when the drive shaft broke. However he managed to join Causeway Lane at speed and steer towards Crown Square where it crashed into the shop and came to rest six feet inside smashing a marble counter and bacon slicer.

Above: A BBC Question Time programme was recorded at Matlock Sunday Night Youth Club in 1952 when questions such as "When should one begin to pay board" and "Are football pools wrong" were discussed. Question master was Jack Longland pictured flanked by team members John Smedley, Florence Renshaw, Beryl Smith and Tom Corbett. Mrs Marjorie Tait (left) is seen asking a question with producer Jack Singleton behind her.

Left: Some of the teenagers who packed Matlock Town Hall for the recording.

Prior to the 1960's racing pigeons had always been sent by rail to their starting point, and here in 1952 members of the Derby, Burton North Road Federation with their baskets of pigeons on Matlock Station are waiting to send their birds to Lerwick in the Shetland Isles – a distance of 485 miles. Nowadays purpose-built transporters going by road do the job, picking birds up from each individual club in the district. Ten owners from Wessington Homing Society sent 27 birds, Bonsall HS 13 sent 33, Wirksworth HS 14 sent 25 and Matlock HS 14 sent 20. In charge of the Matlock marking station was Matlock HS secretary David Day, other stations were at Alfreton and Derby. Among those who sent pigeons were the previous year's winning partnership of Frisby, Keeton and Rawson, with fellow Wessington flyers Calladine Bros., Hill Bros. and. Wheatcroft and Calladine. From Matlock Cyril Yates, Dennis Boden, Roy Furniss, Dan Furniss, Ernie Gratton and Ward and White. Bonsall Bond and Bunting, A Allsop, L Allsop, H Allsop, E Buckley, Bill Waite, Land and Axe, C Roper, J Wood and F and H Loxley. Wirksworth Spencer, Bunting and Gould, Brewell and Higton, Pearson and Cooper, Arthur Killer, F Millward and Peach and Mee.

A new boiler arrived at Smedley's Hydro in Matlock during 1952. Weighing in at a massive 28 tons, the boiler's installation was supervised by Wm. Twigg of Matlock. Two lorries, one in front and one behind, pulled the load to the top of Bank Road which was closed for two days.

December 1955 was a historic date for Derbyshire when Alderman Charles White arrived at Smedley's Hydro in Matlock to accept the keys and formally take possession of the premises. It was the end of months of legal and sometimes bitter wrangling and signalled Derbyshire County Council's move from their headquarters in Derby to Matlock. Pictured as usual with note book and pen in hand is Mrs Ella Smith editor and founder of the Coming Events which later became the Matlock Mercury.

Flying Officer John Clayton – a member of the Matlock Squadron Air Training Corps - salutes at the Pic Tor Cenotaph on the hilly crag above Matlock Dale on Remembrance Day in 1954. Over 20 wreaths were laid by local organisations and the Last Post and Reveille were sounded by six members of Matlock Band.

Highlight of any Matlock Carnival festivity in 1954 was the swimming gala in the town's open-air pool. Crowds here are watching a mop fight while Malcolm Sellers and Alan Andrews hold the platform.

Youngsters queuing for free rides in Santa's sleigh in the run-up to Christmas 1953 – courtesy of Herbert Hardy's Stocking Shop in Crown Square, Matlock. Mr Hardy developed Dene Quarry at Cromford and later founded Direct Furnishing Supplies (DFS) and Two Dales Cara-Hols.

On show to proud parents – these youngsters at Woodlands School on Wellington Street, Matlock, are pictured at the Parents' Day in 1954. They include Kathryn Taylor, Priscilla Bailey, Belinda Jones, Rosemary Upton, Eleanor Dobson, Christine Cook, John Thompson, Richard Wain, Norman Pheasey, David Allen, Margaret Black, Jennifer Black, Michael Platts, Brian Tunnicliffe and Anthea Derbyshire. Earlier the school was situated on Bakewell Road in Matlock and headmistress and founder was Mrs Winifred Dimmock. Formerly Miss Winifred White, she was the sister of Alderman Charles White, and up to its closure the school was always known affectionately as "Miss White's".

Cadets from the 140 (Matlock) Squadron air Cadets spent a memorable week in September 1953 at the RAF Manby Flying College. All cadets had an average of five hours flying in Hastings or Lincoln aircraft, while those with licences flew gliders. They also took part in small-bore rifle shooting, beating cadets from Rolls-Royce and Ashbourne. Flight Lieutenant Raymond Hole was in charge of the Squadron and is pictured (centre) with the cadets in front of a Hastings.

A cousin of Queen Mary opened Matlock All Saints' Church garden party in July 1952. She was Lady May Abel Smith the daughter of the Earl of Athlone and Princess Alice Countess of Athlone. Lady May and Mrs J M Carr, wife of the vicar, were friends in their schooldays. All Saints Girl Guide Margaret Holmes is seen here presenting a bouquet to Lady May in the company of Mrs Carr, Church warden Mr Thomas Taylor and the Rev Carr.

Matlock Bath Carnival Committee chose 21-year-old Miss Lilian Robinson (centre) as their queen for 1951. Her attendants were two 18-year-olds, Miss Sybil Wright (left) and Miss Mavis Bird (right), they are pictured here chatting to Councillor Remo Tinti, Chairman of the committee.

Yvonne Fletcher an 18-year-old sixth form student at the Ernest Bailey Grammar School was chosen as Matlock British Legion Carnival Queen for 1954. She is pictured (front centre) with attendants Ursula Brookhouse on the left and Jean Marsden on the right. Judges were visitors to the district Mr and Mrs Meyneord and Misses C and D Bates, and with them are Stan Collinge (carnival chairman) and Bob Graham (secretary).

The sun shone in 1955 on 21-year-old Gloria Ballington as she was introduced as Matlock British Legion's Carnival Queen to crowds gathered on the Hall Leys Park at the start of the town's carnival celebrations. Pictured at the ceremony which began with a drum head service of dedication are Mr Eric Orridge (president), Mrs E Harris (Women's Section secretary), Marian White (1955 attendant), Mrs F Wildgoose (Women's Section chairman), Ursula Brookhouse (1954 attendant), Revd C H Ferris (Matlock Rector), Mr Robert Graham (secretary): Mavis Bond (1955 attendant), Queen Gloria Ballington, Yvonne Fletcher (1954 Queen), Jean Marsden (1954 attendant), and Kathleen Antliff and Susan Handley (junior attendants).

Derbyshire Townwomen's Guilds staged a historical pageant in June 1952 covering events from Saxon times to the 20th Century at Swanwick Hayes Conference Centre. Twenty-six guilds took part and Matlock and Darley Dale are pictured in their final Victorian tableau and with Mrs Housley as Queen Victoria, and her ladies in waiting Mrs Fletcher and Mrs Kerr.

Life in the Royal Air Force was portrayed by the High Tor Players in November 1952 when they performed "Worm's Eye View" in Matlock Town Hall. On stage are Derrick Redfern, Cyril Hunter, Margaret Slater, Carl Radford, Marie Wright, Fred Shaw, Peter Carley, Guy Butler, Alistair Storey, Nancy Taylor and Michael Leach.

Over 30 members of the Pink Dominoes took part in "Babes in the Wood" in 1954 – a pantomine produced by members of Matlock Bank Methodist Church in their schoolroom. The title roles were played by Susan Wright and Rosemary Briddon and others taking part were Patricia Evans, sisters Edna, Fay and Ann Farnsworth, Kathleen Mosley, Marjorie Boam, Vera Wright, Phyllis Slater, Barbara Cobb, Jean Burnett, Barbara Binney, Pat de Roeck, Jack Wheeldon, Yvonne Evans, C Greenwood, J Grocott, J Holland, L Knowles, B Wragg, B Derbyshire, D Derbyshire, J Kaye, D Douglas, C Elding, K Mosley, J Flint, M Sellers, D Shaw and J Wheeldon.

A touch of Venice came to Matlock in 1952 when the Operatic Society held a Venetian Ball at Lilybank Hydro. Duets from "Night in Venice" were performed by members Clarice Lill and Cora Oliver, Gerald West and Joyce Loverock, while Alistair Storey led the singing of the "Wine" and "Rogues" choruses. Revellers pictured include Gerald West, Tom and Flora Goodwin, Cedric Smalley, Pamela Haslam, Irene Glew, Cyril Hunter, Alistair Storey, Gwen and Kathleen Chadwick, Peter Eaton, Peter and Mrs Carley and Neil Kerr. Prior to the Ball, the Society had performed "Night in Venice" at the Cinema House but despite good attendances the show made a loss of £140.

Over 90 members and guests attended the fifth Charter Anniversary dinner of Matlock Ladies' Circle at the Ashover Hotel. Circle chairman Mrs Ida Allen is pictured receiving Mrs Barbara Hadfield, supported by Area Chairman Mrs J M Hain, Mrs A V Harrison, Mr Bill Allen and Mr Peter Hadfield.

Over 100 former scholars of the Ernest Bailey Grammar School in Matlock attended a reunion buffet dance at the Lilybank Hydro. President of the Old Bailean Association, Mr B C Orme (headmaster) attended and arrangements were made by Mr Peter Wright with Mr Harold Bradbury acting as MC.

In the January of 1955 Matlock Junior Band were hitting the high notes under conductor Fred Slater as they pose with their trophies. Left to right (back row): Murray Slater, John Garlick, John Slater, Stuart Ashworth, John Vallance, Ken Argent and Les Bradbury: (middle row) John Towe, Alan Woodhouse, John Kersey, Fred Slater, Alwyn Bird, Michael Lowe and Doug Kirkland; (front row) Michael Jackson and Ralph Marsden.

Old Baileans got together at the Lilybank Hotel, Matlock in 1954, for a dinner-dance Some of those pictured enjoying themselves are Keith Beardow, Geoffrey Atkin, Mavis Bird, John Finney, Jenny Green, Haydn and Eunice Kingman, Alistair and Pat Storey, Ann Beastall, George Jenkins, Debbie Eldridge, Cynthia Hollins, Irene Glew, Cedric Smalley, Ray Boden, Neil Kerr, Rosemary Smith, Harry Daniel, Lew Finney, Joan Simcock, Arthur and Peggy Watson, David Loverock, Geoff Henshaw and "Woodbasher" Wootton.

Taking time out from acting in 1954 are these members of the High Tor Players at their annual dinner at High Tor Guest House on Matlock's Artists' Corner. Among them are Mr & Mrs Alistair Storey, Mr & Mrs John Broome, Mr Derrick Redfern, Councillor Mrs A M Greatorex, Mrs Ella Smith, Mr Peter Eaton and Captain L H Morgan (Church Army).

Matlock Junior Band was in the prizes at Sheepbridge Band's annual junior contest in March 1952. Under their conductor Mr Fred Slater the junior quartet took the silver trophy and first place with their rendering of Dudley Buck's Hymn to Music. Murray Slater won the senior solo playing second cornet, Brian Wall came third in the junior solo section on euphonium while Brian Wildgoose won a third with a tenor horn solo. Keith Sheldon, playing with Darley Dale Band, took a second prize. Left to right (back row) are Brian Wall, Fred Slater and Murray Slater; (front) Brian Wildgoose and Ken Argent.

A twice-weekly "battle" which had gone on for 30 years in Matlock Liberal Club was about to be ended in 1954. Bob Newman, Jack Bunting, Herbert Farnsworth and John Hunting had played either cribbage or snooker together since 1925. Bob and Herbert used to challenge all-comers to play them at any game and eventually the other two decided to join them in friendly rivalry – a rivalry which had stood the test of time. The nods and knowing winks were about to end though for Mr Hunting, Head of Bonsall Boys' School, was about to retire and return to his roots in Long Eaton. Mr Newman was former Head of All Saints' School in Matlock, Mr Bunting was manager of Burgon's in Crown Square and Mr Farnsworth was with J W Wildgoose Ltd.

Those really were the days... Matlock Business & Professional Women's Club members Miss B M Statham, Miss M Turner and Mrs A Gentle entertained at the New Year party in 1955. Miss Turner was Matron at the Whitworth Hospital. The trio are also pictured in the group that includes Mrs Marjorie Wardman and Mrs Gladys Wardman. The larger group picture shows members with their president Mrs Winifred A Dimmock, founder of Woodlands School, Matlock and sister of Alderman Charles White.

A Matlock branch of the Royal Air Force Association was inaugurated in 1952 at a meeting at the King's Head Inn, Matlock Town. Philip Mann was elected secretary, George Wardman treasurer, Fred Holmes chairman, and Harold Bradbury vice-chairman. The Association was open to all ex-Service officers, airmen and airwomen and it was proposed to meet every Friday at the King's Head.

Air Cadets from Matlock 140 Squadron spent a week at a Fighter Command station in the summer of 1952. Nineteen teenagers enjoyed flights, shooting and the odd bit of swimming in the sea off the Norfolk coast. Looking after them were Fl. Lt. Raymond Hole, Flying Officer L. Hunt and Pilot Officer J Clayton. Among those pictured with the officers are Cadets Ken Attwater, Terry Kay, Barry Kay, Brian Phillips, David Crapper, Eric Durward, Terry Moore, Edward Huntington and Patrick Cafferty.

Judges, officials and exhibitors are pictured at the first-ever show of the Matlock and District Poultry Keepers' Club which was held in the Whitworth Institute at Darley Dale in February 1954.

The Matlock and District Building Trades Employers Association held its annual dinner and social at Ye Olde Englishe Hotel in February 1954 when the president Mr L W Wildgoose was in the chair. Guests pictured include representatives from Lehane, Mackenzie and Shand Ltd, Matlock Building Supplies Ltd, Permanite Ltd., William Twigg Ltd. and Matlock Urban District Council.

The Church Army had always been a strong force in the Matlock area with headquarters on Matlock Green. Probably the most popular leader was Captain Morgan (centre front) seen here in 1955 with his wife at their farewell dinner at Lilybank Hydro before their move to Retford. Captain Morgan received a brief case from members of the Sunday Night Youth Club which he helped to establish. After its closure some years later the HQ was sold and became known as Tawney House.

There was a good turnout of members of Matlock Young Farmers' Club when they met to see chairman Malcolm Statham (left) receive a new trophy for the club. It was the Silcock Trophy and was handed over by Mr Arthur Watson (right) in memory of his late father. Pictured with them are members and officials including Derek Holmes, Miss Sybil Lennox, Mr and Mrs Frank Statham, Mr Tom Marshall, Mr George Lomas, Mr Fred Hole, Graham Marshall, Harry Walker, John Holmes, Ed Marchant, Bill Quinlan, Ernest Marchant, Bridget Neville, Margaret Hawkins and Lucy Brown.

Happy Scouts, Guides and Cubs attended the 15th Matlock (Starkholmes) Scout Group's annual party in February 1954 in the Matlock Green Church Army Social Centre. Some of the Guides were from Gedling in Nottingham and who had shared a campsite at Chapel St Leonards the previous year. The Parents' committee served tea and MC for the party was Scoutmaster Reg Ross.

Miss White, a guest at the Matlock Business & Professional Women's club party, January 1955

In the same year Matlock Town Football Club were playing in the Central Alliance and some of the players in their squad are pictured here, including Don Spencer, Alf Manship, Frank Wildgoose, Alan Perry, George Boden, Frank Middleton and – Wetton.

All Saints School, Matlock, won the South Peak Schools athletic sports on Causeway Lane ground in 1952. Headmaster Mr Jack Hunt and Councillors George Slade and Thomas Johnson are pictured with trophy winners Marion Taylor, Patricia Hagues, Ann Farnsworth, Ralph Marsden, Derek Barker and Maurice Bailey.

Derwent House won the Greatorex Cup at Matlock Town School's annual sports in 1952 when Mrs C H Ferris, wife of the Rector of Matlock, made the presentations. With her are captains Michael Oxley and Kathleen Greatorex and high jump winners Geoffrey Hulley and Margaret Whitworth.

Senior Champions.

Highlight of swimming galas in the district was the annual South Peak Senior and Junior Schools championships. Winner of the 1954 Junior event was Matlock All Saints team consisting of Roger Chamberlain, Michael Land, M Riley, B Moore, Gwyneth Holmes, J Vallance and Susan Wright. Senior champions were the Ernest Bailey Grammar School represented by Dennis Farnsworth, J Woodley, B Wilson, Roger Gedye, G Hunt, Rosemary Holmes, Marcia Young, G Richards, Ian Stuart, J Vallance, Diane Soppitt, Jean Askew and P Wilson.

Junior Champions.

In 1954 the Danes team won for the third consecutive year the girls' House championship in the Ernest Bailey Grammar School sports on Cromford Meadows. Pictured with House Mistress Pamela Hubbard are left to right, back row Marguerite Hetherington, Mary Locke (captain), Jacqueline Tindall, Glenys Evans and Marcia Young; front row Marion Wall, Janet Smith, Sylvia Taylor and Joan Flint.

Pictured after the Ernest Bailey Grammar School speech day in 1954 are these scholars who include Judith Gregory, Hans Espig, John Standen, Ian Callard, Kenneth Bowler, Ann Horobin, Shirley and Sheila Smith, Marilyn Lane, Mary Locke, Jacqueline Tindall, Cynthia Wright, Shirley Robinson, Brenda Soppitt, Aileen Crookes, Peter Morris.

Headmaster and conductor of South Darley School choir Wilf Warren is pictured in June 1954 with scholars at Matlock Bath Music Festival. They had just won the first prize in the under-12 class for choral verse speaking and are left to right (back row) David Jaina, Robert Winthrope, Richard Beck, Maurice Knill, Ramon Else, David Pritty and John Arnold, (middle row) John Cauldwell, Alan Ainsworth, John Wright, Norman Concannon, Bryan Wildgoose and Ian Fearn, (front row) Mary Dunn, Jane Arnold, Susan Goodison, Irene Wheeldon, Maureen Devaney, Mary Widdison, Janet Dunn and Fay Wildgoose.

The Charles White Secondary School in Matlock was the venue in September 1958 for a conference designed to welcome 72 first-year students who had just joined Derbyshire County Council schools. Among them was Mrs Elma Williams, an exchange teacher from Los Angeles who was joining Matlock County Infants School, Miss Joyce Allen, of Matlock, going to Cromford C of E School and Mr Frank Orrery, newly-appointed science master at Anthony Gell Grammar School, Wirksworth. Pictured (left to right) are Mr Orrery, Alderman Mrs Gladys Buxton (Chairman of the County Council), Mr Jack Longland (Education Director), Alderman F A Gent (Chairman of the Education Committee), Mrs Williams and Miss Allen.

The gymnasium at Matlock Presentation Convent High School provided in 1953 the venue for St Joseph's Catholic Church Sunday School party. Children enjoyed indoor sports, competitions and a tea provided by the nuns.

The younger generation gave an outstanding performance in "The Rising Generation" in March 1954 when the Ernest Bailey Grammar School produced their annual play in Matlock Town Hall. From left to right are Valerie Watkinson, Barrie Boden, Pauline Hare, Valerie Jackson, John Elliott, Kenneth Bowler, Daphne Stevens, Joan Hammond, John Standen, Geoffrey Slater and David Greenhough.

Scholars and staff of Matlock County School took over the Town Hall in March 1954 for two nights to perform their original panto "Old London Town" written by Headmaster Tom Varnam. All scenery was built in the school woodwork room under the supervision of Mr Bernard Taylor and which was designed and painted by Mr Charles Berry. The costumes were lent by Mr Herbert Hardy, of The Stocking Shop in Crown Square and dancer Pamela Nightingale devised and arranged her own repertoire. Pictured are some of the cast (left to right) Michael Jackson, Tony Stoppard, Hazel Walker, June Ward, Mr George Boden, Peggy Baldwin, Pamela Nightingale, Roy Salt, Keith Briddon, Mary Jones and Carol Barker.

Police constable Len Lea, captain of Matlock Police cricket team holds the H E Giles knock-out trophy which the team retained for the second year. With him are Sgt Noel Bishop, Sgt John Anderson, PC Ray Ogden, PC Stuart Oliver, PC Albert Tattersall, DC Arthur Willis, Sgt David Burgoyne, PC Eric Bottom, PC Jack Robinson and PC Eric Lipscombe.

Proud smiles from these members of Matlock Golf Club in October, 1950, on winning the Derbyshire Inter-club championships. Left to right are Richard Wragg, Archie Hill, Harold Swindell (captain), Lewis Edwards and Joe Worthy who are pictured with the Duke of Devonshire Cup.

The finals of the Matlock and District Darts League knockout competitions were held at the Boat House Hotel, Matlock in 1952, when Mr L W Wildgoose presented the trophies. League champions Three Stags, Darley Bridge, runners-up Grouse Inn 'A', Darley Dale; Pairs left-right: Hopkinson and B Waller (Three Stags), runners-up S Quigley and K Hardy (Three Stags); Captains competition H Woodhouse (Three Stags), runner-up S Bagshaw (Queen's Head); Ladies competition Mrs Davey and Miss Dooley (Red Lion, Matlock), runners-up Mrs Gill and Mrs Frost (Boat House, Matlock).

There was a shock result in the finals of the Matlock Local Table Tennis championships in 1954 when reigning champion Joy Dakin was defeated by Rosemary Smith 21-14, 14-21, 20-22. in the ladies' final. In the Veteran Men's Jack Ridgard, undefeated in the League, had to be content with a runner-up trophy. Officials, trophy winners and some of the other players are pictured, including Ian Wheeldon, David Ridgard, Leo White, Ken Boitoult, David Ollerenshaw, Gordon Andrews, Max Holmes, Steve Bunting, Geoff Hurst, Doug Fearn, Horace Gratton and Matthew Bunting.

A record entry of over 100 competitors took part in the second annual tennis tournament organised by Matlock Attractions Committee in 1952. Pictured on the Hall Leys courts included chairman J E Moreton seen here chatting to, among others, Andy Duncan, Peter Fearn, Capt Morgan (Church Army), Tony Bond and Alan Kingman.

The second North Derbyshire Badminton League championships were held in Matlock Bath Parochial Hall early in 1954. Finalists posing for this picture are: back row (left to right) Ken Black, Barbara Marsden, Betty Sharpe, Ann Steward, Edna Bevan, Evelyn Roberts, Eileen Burnett and Jenny Green; front row Eric Bevan, Geoff Tym and Matthew Bunting.

At Matlock Cycling Club's annual dinner in 1954 Graham Bland was awarded the accolade of Best All Rounder for 1953. Among the other awards he received from the hands of Brian Robinson who wore the leader's jersey for three days in the previous year's Tour of Britain, were F L White BAR Shield, Hawksworth Mountain Time Trial Cup, Hawksworth TT Cup for Darley Dale to Cannock and Back, Hill Climb Cup, Plaque for Most Improved Rider, 25-mile TT winner, 30-mile TT winner and Mountain TT winner. Brian Robinson is on the left next to club president Walter Kerr, Mr A P Chamberlin (National Cyclists' Union representative) and Graham.

Matlock Cycling Club held their third annual dinner at the Fishpond Hotel in 1955 when Ray Booty, Britain's leading cyclist, was guest of honour. Among his many successes was 1st in the Isle of Man Road Race, 1st Bath 100 miles Time Trial, 2nd in the British Best All-rounder competition and member of the British team in the World Road Race championships. After dinner Mr Booty went on to present trophies won by the Matlock cyclists and he is pictured (third from left) with Albert Renshaw, Brian Slater, Graham Bland, Dennis Hawley, Bill Brentnall and Philip Taylor. Graham was main senior prizewinner, taking the Club BAR Trophy, Cannock and Back Trophy, Buxton and Back Trophy, Hill Climb Trophy, Mountain Time Trial Trophy and fastest 10-mile TT Plaque.

Pictured at their ground on Cromford Meadows in 1953 are the Old Baileans Rugby Club's 1st XV. Left to right (back row) Des Charlton, Doug Tembey, Dick Caudwell, Roland Oliver, Graham Ellis, David Loverock, Les Bowler, Eugene McNevin, Des Marsden and Harold Bradbury: (front row) Geoff Wildgoose, Haydn Kingman, Ron Broome, Bob Stafford, Les Steele and Trevor Tuffin.

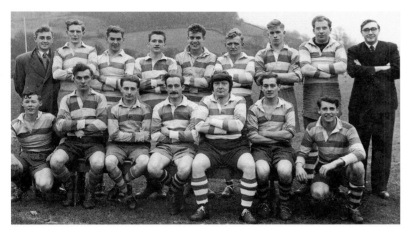

The Old Baileans 2nd XV played the Ernest Bailey Grammar School and ran out winners by 6 points to 3. Pictured are: back row (left to right) John Finney, Keith Marsden, Geoff Slater, Alan Teece, Terry Kay, Haydn Kingman, David Ramsden, Paul Dolton, John Hancock; front row Alan Ball, Sid Quigley, Ron Duggins, Alan Fletcher, Max Holmes, Keith Bagshaw and Gordon Statham.

The Old Baileans 2nd XV team pictured at the end of the 1957–58 season are: Back row (left to right) Gordon Statham, Joe Smith, Mike Boswell, John Slater, Graham Twigg, Pat Cafferty, Ian Shaw, Terry Boswell, John Marsden and Dennis Hooton; (front row) Brian Ball, Bob Stafford, Sid Quigley, Keith Bagshaw, John Hooton, Lew Finney.

No competitive games were played by the Ernest Bailey Grammar School, Matlock, rugby team in 1955, but they did play ten friendlies which they won. Taken on their pitch at Cromford Meadows this picture shows left to right (back row): John West, Brian Clarke, Mick Paulson, Roger Gedye, David Fearn, Derek Allwood, Max Burkimsher and Dennis Farnsworth; (front row) John Seedhouse, Peter Lomas, Peter Holland, Wally Redfern, Mick Marsden, Alan Greenhough and Tommy Walker.

A close-fought game against Derby RUFC 'A' saw the Old Baileans 1st XV go down by 3 points to 5 on Cromford Meadows in December 1955. Captain John Billingham (centre front) is pictured with other members Graham Twigg, Dick Standen, David Loverock, Conrad Loeber, Ray Boden, Colin Greatorex, Pat Cafferty, Harry Daniel, Gerald Newton, Haydn Kingman (referee), Bob Stafford, Graham Ellis, Trevor Tuffin and Geoff Lomas.

Ladies football was popular in 1955 and several teams took part in Matlock British Legion's carnival that year. The final game took place between Northwood Ladies and Hooley Estate on the Causeway Lane ground. From the start Northwood were the better team, but an injury to a Hooley player reduced their team to ten and so it came as no surprise when Mavis Parker opened the scoring and then added another before the interval. June Gannicott made it 3-0 to Northwood after the interval and so received their trophy from Carnival Queen Gloria Ballington. The Northwood team pictured with trainer Jack Stevenson and manager Dinah Twigg are Hazel Marsden, Mary Cope, Rose Horobin, Eileen Burnett, Hazel Kinder, Kathleen Parkey, Elizabeth Kent, June Gannicott, Hazel Marsden, Mary Parker and Marie Wilson.

The Hooley Estate Ladies team in 1955 were formidable opponents and they included Beryl King, Hazel Flint, Daphne Cundy, June Wardle, – Wood, "Razzer" Goodwin (manager), Mary Greatorex, Edna Hill, Noreen Teece, – Baker, Joyce Mellor and Lilian Waterfall.

Three championship titles were won by Matlock Swifts in the 1953-54 season. They became the first Matlock team to win the Rowsley and District Youth League, won the Benevolent Cup and the DFA Junior Medals (Matlock and Buxton Division). Swifts played 30 League and Trophy matches and lost only three – all at the hands of Bonsall. Pictured are Barry Mackay, Raymond Grindey, Brian Wall (captain), Philip Sellers, David Slack, David Ramsden, Gerald Newton, Bernard Maskrey, David McDowell, Alan Stevenson, Philip Sellers, Roy Blackham and George Sellers (trainer).

The 1955/6 football season began in fine style for Matlock Town. They won their opening home game against British Ropes in the Central Alliance by two goals to nil, and the following Wednesday defeated Derby County 'A' 3-6 at Sinfin Lane. Pictured are some of the players who include (left to right) J Roberts, Jack Wragg, Alf Manship, Bill Rhodes, Michael Howard, Peter Howe, A Elton, Mr L F Butler (manager); seated T Abbey, J Hallam, J Lakin, Colin Leatherday and D Green.

Easter football in Matlock kicked off to a poor start when the Town Reserves went down by two goals to one on Good Friday morning in the final of the DFA Divisional Cup (North) against Heanor Reserves. Supporters pose with the team in this picture which includes Maureen and Mrs Whitworth, Harry Marian, Cyril Harrison, Mrs Cynthia Harvey, Jasper Wright, Millard, Miller, Quinn, Holmes, Leggett, Noble, Buxton, Thompson, Rose, Furniss and Hall.

Early-season trials for a place in Matlock Town's team squad proved embarrassing for officials. Ex-professionals, semi-professionals and locals were all eager to show-off their talents to the selection committee on the Rowsley ground. Referee was Ken Britland, of Wirksworth, and he is pictured with players Whitam, Jessop, Spence, Newberry, Doxey, Shingler, Alan Briggs, Boyes, Siddall, Howard, Herring, Beastall, Watkinson, Webb, Boden, Poole, McGowan, George Eaton, Frank Eaton, Mick Betteridge, Bull and Roberts.

Derbyshire Stone Football Club posed for this picture at the start of the 1953/54 season. Back row: Frank Booth (secretary), Bill Askew, Syd Smith, Ken Mellor, Peter Yates, Frank Wildgoose, Brian Phillips, Arthur Millward, Gordon Maskrey; (front row) Harry Goodall, Tom Matkin, Geoff Carline, Paul Maskrey (mascot), Steve Bunting and Jack McCann.

Middleton by Wirksworth

A dance organised by Middleton-by-Wirksworth coronation committee in 1952 raised money for one of the village's footballers who broke his leg in the first match of the season. Carnival trophies were presented by queen Gillian Hayes to Mrs A Petts (ladies football, Duke of Wellington), Mr L Flint (cricket cup, Middleton Institute), Runners-up Miss S Benyon (Smithy team) and Mr L Marshall (Middleton CC) received cash prizes which were handed back the fund. Mrs Ella Smith presided over the evening and arrangements were made by Councillors L and Hubert Doxey.

When it came to blowing their own trumpet Middleton (by Wirksworth) Victoria Silver Prize Band were the tops. William Samuel Spencer founded the Band in 1897, the year of Queen Victoria's Diamond Jubilee, and other Middleton men who played in the Wirksworth Volunteer Band joining him as founder members were Messrs W Jones, E Mather, G Killer, J Doxey, David Brocklehurst, Henry, Josiah, John and William Slack, S Brooks, T Buckley and W Spencer. Mr William Samuel Spencer wielded the baton until 1923 when he handed over to his son Joseph Samuel who was killed in a quarrying accident in 1953. Taken in 1954, this picture shows (back row) Vincent Haymes, Jack Houghton, Keith Jepson, Doug Tomlinson (secretary), Jim Haymes, George Holmes, Russell Southam, Ian Hayes, Barry Gratton, Jack Houghton junr, Dick Slack (assistant conductor), Alf Higton, Ron Brooks, William Statham, Sam Pearson, Jack Haymes and Alan Doxey, (front row) Peter Gratton, Isaac Gratton, John Samuel Batterley (treasurer), Jim Beeson, Matthew Haymes (bandmaster), L W (Billy) Wildgoose (conductor), Doug Wood, Isaac Spencer and Cedric Pearson.

Rowsley

Rowsley School brought out the silverware for their annual sports day when Lord John Manners presented the prizes and trophies. He is in the centre of the picture and Headmaster Mr Wilfred Holland is third from the left with the Rev. C Storrs Fox next to him. Trophy winners were (left to right) Donald Carter, John Pennington, Hazel Marsden, Elizabeth Kent, George Mansfield and Diana Allsop. Two new trophies were presented to past scholars Hazel and George by former teacher Miss Gladys Hallows (fourth from right).

Headmaster Wilf Holland and some of his staff and children are pictured in 1953 at Rowsley School's Christmas dinner in the Village Hall.

Civil engineers Lehane, Mackenzie and Shand Ltd of Rowsley and Darley Dale, held their first annual dinner at the New Bath Hotel, Matlock Bath, in 1953. The occasion was a double celebration for the previous week Digley Reservoir had been opened by Huddersfield Corporation and which had been built by the company. Joint managing directors Mr A T B ("Sandy") Shand and Mr N C S Meares (back row) are pictured with guests Major M H S Meares, Mrs S D Shand, Mrs H M S Meares, Mrs N C S Meares, Mrs and Mr G R Gascoyne.

All aboard the steam train with driver Arnold Milnes at the controls, VIPs at a Conservative Rally at Haddon Hall took a trip round the grounds. They include (from right) Anthony Nutting MP, E B Wakefield MP, the Duke of Rutland, the Duke of Devonshire, Lord John Manners and Col. J F Crompton-Inglefield.

A man taking stone from local quarries to help secure the breached sea defences at Chapel St Leonards suffered only a sprained wrist when his lorry left the A6 and crashed on to the railway line at Rowsley. Mr Dennis Robinson, of Hartington, was lucky to escape so lightly when his lorry struck a stationary railway wagon.

Starkholmes

There were Maypole and country dancers at Starkholmes May Festival in June 1954 when Maureen Whitworth was crowned as Queen by Mrs F W Beddington. Councillor Mrs A M Greatorex presided and was accompanied by Mrs E C P Stevens. Attending Maureen were Helen Sims and Jennifer Bean and bouquets were presented by Beverley Beacon. Dancers pictured with the Festival Royalty are Sheila Simms, Angela Blackham, Dorothy Martin, Linda Boswell, Ellie Kirk, Beverely Beacon, Barbara Fletcher, Gillian Allsop, Patricia Meneaud, Janet Boswell, Margaret and Lilian Grocott, Olive Wilson, Margaret Armory, Susan Allen, Margaret Shaw, Dorothy Parker, Judy Hallam, Ann Allsop, Gloria and Patricia Fearn.

An attack of mumps prevented 14-year-old Judith Hallam from being crowned Starkholmes May Queen in 1955, but two months later she more than made up for the disappointment when she was crowned Carnival Queen by Mrs S Tomlinson. Alderman John Turner, vice-chairman of Matlock Urban District Council officially opened the event, under the watchful eye of life-president Cyril Harrison. Also pictured are Mrs Turner, Mrs Warren, chairman John Fern, Mrs Fearn, Elizabeth Bollington, Gillian Allsop, Ellie Kirk, Gillian Statham, Judith Statham, Barbara Haynes, Ann Flint, Anne Allsop and Mary Allsop.

Miss Shirley Rhodes was crowned Starkholmes Carnival Queen for 1954 by Mrs Kenneth Drabble at a ceremony on the recreation ground. Mrs Drabble was introduced by life president Cyril Harrison, who is pictured with Chairman John Fern, retiring Queen Isobel Spencer, Josie Warren, Ellie Kirk, Gillian Allsop, Beverley Beacon, Olive Wilson, Sheila and Olive Simms, Barbara Fletcher, Angela Blackham, Mary Allsop, Dorothy Martin, Susan Hallam and Pat Clayton.

Passing the parcel – Councillor Eric Stevens caught in 'possession' at Starkholmes Village Hall annual dinner and social on 20th March 1954.

Tansley

Youngsters from the Brunswick Methodist Sunday School at Tansley took to the stage when they performed "Babes in the Wood". Playing the Babes were Maureen Wills and Richard Hilton and they are pictured with Birds Lyn Jamieson, Valerie Brailsford, Ada Kirk, Susan Briddon, Andrea Harding, Barbara Slack and Christine Knowles.

In 1954 councillor Eric Stevens and Matlock Urban District Clerk Norman Brook and his wife chose Miss Mary Whittaker (second from right, front row) as Tansley Carnival Queen. Attendants Miss Dorothy Perkins and Miss June Gregory and 1953 Queen Pamela Haslam are pictured with them along with Eric Acton (Parish Hall treasurer), Mrs J Wills (secretary) and Dennis Birch (chairman).

Tansley Carnival Queen Miss Pamela Haslam looked resplendent at the village carnival in 1953. She is seen here with attendants Miss Audrey Briddon and Miss Lucy Brown.

Mrs C F White crowned Mrs Margaret Lomas as queen of Tansley carnival on the village green in 1952. Mrs Lomas was attended by Miss Mary Whittaker and Miss Audrey Briddon and train-bearer Miss Patricia Cook They are pictured with Mr Eric Acton (treasurer), Alderman C F White, Mr Bert Briddon, Miss Shirley Froggatt attendant to retiring queen Miss Margaret Bunting who is on the extreme right.

Tansley carnival queen in 1951 was Miss Margaret Bunting (centre) with Miss Shirley Froggatt (left) and Miss Joyce Acton (right) as her attendants.

Two Dales

The Two Dales Nag's Head Homing Society dinner and prize presentation in 1954 attracted 55 guests to their headquarters. Matlock Urban District councillors and their wives joined club president Joe Allwood and his wife Mary for the meal and entertainment which included a Derbyshire dialect poem by club member Tom Concannon about when his pigeon flew down a well-known personalities' chimney. Main award, the Combined Average Cup, was presented to Graham Brookhouse (centre right) by Mrs Allwood (Mr Allwood is between them) as well as the Old Bird Average. Jack Gill won the Young Bird Average and other prizewinners were Frank Byard and Son, Arnold Webster, Harry Witham, Len Evans, Fred Bannister, Tom Concannon, Eric Bannister, Jack Carter, George Boden, Harry Evans, Wilburn Boam and Jimmy Slack.

Wensley

Wensley Football Club enjoyed a happy Easter in 1955 when they won the Bakewell Cup, qualified for the final of the Bakewell Junior Cup and the semi-finals of the Cavendish Cup. The team and officials pictured include Neville Siddall, Les Masters, David Devaney, Harry Taylor, Cyril Howes, Bill Richardson, Ray Howes, G Wragg, R Spencer, Fred Rogers, Peter Sellors, Eric Wright, Bernard Cooper, Max Dakin, Don Marsden, Harold Grimshaw and Tony Evans.

Wensley Red Star Football Club won the Bakewell Cup and the Bakewell League Cup in the 1951-52 season...and both trophies shared pride of place on the top table at the club's annual dinner in the Crown Inn, Wensley. Members of the team were (back row) Peter Yates (goalkeeper); (middle row) Bill Jordan, Graham Brookhouse, Dennis Allwood, Peter Sellors, Brian Boam; (front row) Bernard Cooper, Ivan Greatorex, Doug Ryder, Bill Richardson and Tony Evans. Originally, Red Star played down Wensley Dale, but later they used the Derbyshire Stone pitch off Snitterton Road.

Derbyshire Stone FC managed to raise a smile despite being beaten 4-0 by Wensley in a Bakewell and District League match early in September 1955. Pictured are (standing left to right) Frank Booth (secretary), Ken Harrison, Sid Smith, Peter Lowe, George Carline, Brian Wall, Bob Rouse, Len Lees (assistant trainer), Jack Bick (vice-chairman and trainer): (front row) Pat Turner (referee), Gerald Paine, Des Andrews, Brian Phillips, Bob Wood and George Dakin.

Winster

Winster Main Street was closed on Shrove Tuesday 1952 as housewives took part in the pancake-tossing race…but there were so many entrants it had to be split into four heats. The final was won by Mrs Kathleen Greatorex, followed by Miss A Thorneycroft, Mrs J Spencer and Mrs H Webster. Mrs Spencer is mother of Mrs Greatorex and her granddaughter Pat was first in the children's shuttlecock race. Roland Corfield and Marion Stone were runners-up. Mr Horace Johnson, who was responsible for the revival of this annual event, was organiser and also donated the prizes.

Another two years had passed but tradition goes on. More pancake racers get ready at Winster in 1954 for the line-up, including Barry Fairey, Sam Marsden, Annie Slaney, Monica Stone, Amy Slater, Philip Willett, Evelyn Nutt, Eileen Slater and Kathleen Spencer.

Morris dancers from Cambridge, Nottingham and Derbyshire joined forces at Winster Wakes celebrations in 1952 for a festival of dancing. The 60-odd performers danced their way along Main Street to Oddo Park, stopping to dance outside the home of 94-year-old James Marshall, the Winster Morris Dancers first 'queen.'

Adding a touch of humour to Winster Wakes in August 1954 were the hilariousHoward–Morten Carnival Circus who were based at Cromford.

When characters meet…Ben Clay (left) and Edwin Newton. Barrow-boy Ben hit the national headlines in 1954 when he and his barrow loaded with fruit and veg were barricaded in Matlock Park Head by Matlock Urban District Council when they were in dispute over street trading. Edwin was Winster's oldest resident, being born in the village in 1861 and among the first pupils at Winster School.

Residents of Winster still remember the day in 1952 when the earth moved for them and shattered the peace of this ancient mining village. Walls bulged and cracked, ceilings came down and chimneys were left leaning crazily. The date was February 22nd and the time 9.20 am. A massive earth tremor brought people running from their homes into the street where rubble covered footpaths, which had been full of children walking to school only 20 minutes earlier. Was it an explosion, a landslip, a mine collapse or was it a good old-fashioned earthquake. Those were some of the questions posed as villagers compared their experiences. Butcher Fred Blackwell said his wife was terrified and ran outside when a chimney stack fell down, radio dealer Vinny Hodgkinson claimed he heard two bangs and Joe Smith said the ground seemed to roll under his feet. Bill Slaney said he could hear water rushing under Main Street, he also claimed Mrs Bertha Stone, landlady of the Crown Inn, was sitting on the edge of her bed when the shock wave threw her on to the floor. Mrs Slaney was walking past Woolley's Yard when a chimneystack crashed to the ground and Mrs Mavis Corker and her mother Mrs Sarah Wilson were in their home Carpenter's Cottage on Main Street. "Mum had just gone into the kitchen to put a shilling in the gas meter when there was a tremendous bang. I thought she had blown herself up so I ran towards the kitchen only to be met by her running out shouting 'Get out, get out, the house is falling down!' She thought I had wrongly lit the gas stove and had blown myself up." The following month a high-powered deputation arrived in Winster to listen to the villagers' fears, they included Alderman Charles White, Chairman of Derbyshire County Council, Clerk Dennis Gilman and Mr Stanley Clift, Geological Research Officer. Pictured with them outside the Market Hall are Parish Councillors Horace Johnson (chairman) and Harry Boden, Clerk Harry Needham, the Rev B T Abel, PC Frank Hannigan and news reporter Sam Fay. Mr Clift spent a week in Winster and declared the village was built on the most solid rock imaginable and that the tremor area had extended over 13 square miles.

Wirksworth

Pretty as a picture these young maypole dancers from Wirksworth were due to give a display in June 1953 at Bolehill WI's field day in the afternoon, but rain washed out their performance. However they were able to perform in the town later that day.

Ringing in the New Year of 1953 and celebrating the Coronation at Wirksworth St Mary's Church were this team of 'veterans' – Ben Johnson with 53 years' service, Brian Hilditch (50), Frank Johnson (60) years and Laurie Hanson (56).

A Medal depicting the centenary of the Derbyshire Mining Customs and Mineral Courts Act of 1852 was struck and presented to the Queen. It was presented by H J Enthoven and Sons Ltd and smelted from lead ore supplied by Derbyshire Stone Ltd. The Arms of the Duchy of Lancaster as depicted on the Queen's County Palatine Seal were approved by the Chancellor of the Duchy to denote the Royal connection. Admiring the medal at a meeting of the Wirksworth Barmote Court in the Moot Hall are (left to right) Councillor Mrs A M Greatorex (chairman of Matlock Urban District Council), her daughter Miss Jean Greatorex, Mr Kenneth L Cobb (chairman H J Enthoven and Sons Ltd), Major J D B Symonds (Barmote Court Steward) and Mr George Edwin Bacon (Barmote Court Foreman).

"Absolutely the last word in fire engines" was how Derbyshire's chief fire officer Mr A I Galloway described Wirksworth's new appliance when it was commissioned in 1953. Costing £3250 the machine was handed over by Alderman R Fewkes, chairman of Derbyshire County Council fire brigade committee. At the ceremony, Councillor Fred Slater, chairman of Wirksworth Urban District Council, recalled how in the early days the town was served by a horse-drawn fire appliance that was kept in the Market Place, and the first man to bring horses to the appliance after the fire bell had rung was given ten shillings. Standing by the 120 hp Dennis F8 machine are Chief Fire Officer Galloway, Councillors Slater, Arthur Hallow, Norman Harrison, Reg Brewer, Hubert Doxey, Alderman Fewkes, Wirksworth Water Engineer Bill Webber, Councillors Jack Slack, C W (Jimmy) James, Veronica Stafford and George Thompson.

Popping in for a quick one took on a whole new meaning for the driver of this lorry when it ran into the Hope and Anchor public house in Wirksworth in May 1954. Local driver Mr E Dexter managed to jump clear before the impact.

Forty years of service to Haarlem Mill at Wirksworth was recognised in 1955 by employees when they said farewell to director and secretary Lieutenant Colonel C J Wheatcroft. He and his wife were presented on behalf of the employees with a radio by works manager Mr Douglas Tomlinson who wished them well on their retirement to Devonshire. They are pictured with Mr and Mrs Kenneth Wheatcroft and Mr and Mrs Michael Wheatcroft.

A record number of Old Wirksworthian Association members crowded into the gym at the Anthony Gell Grammar School for their annual reunion dance in 1955. Arrangements were made by the committee with Mr Brian Haworth as chairman, Mr Maitland Hilditch secretary and Mr Peter Sutton treasurer. Some of the happy revellers pictured include Mary Fritchley, Roger Hargreaves, Mary Buxton, Brenda Gallimore, George Rowland, Joy Coates, Elspeth Gallimore and Connie Rowland.

The Rotary Club of Wirksworth's inaugural meeting was held on October 23, 1947, and Frederick Vincent Stirland, manager of the town's Westminster Bank, was elected president. Eleven years later a good number attended the annual Charter Dinner under the leadership of President Philip Cash. The club had 22 members, many of whom are pictured here with guests from other clubs. The membership comprised Bernard Ash (treasurer), Herbert Astill, Ralph Blackwall, Sidney Chalmers (secretary), Philip Cash, Harold Eccleshare, Leslie Fletcher, George Guise, William Hatfield (honorary member), John Hall, Harold Haworth, Reg Jennings, Frank Milner, Benjamin Payne, Norman Perrin, Fred Read, Phillip Slater, George Taylor, Douglas Tomlinson, Samuel Wardman, Gerald Witham and Leonard Yeomans (vice-president).

Another highlight in Wirksworth's social calendar was the police annual ball in the Town Hall in April 1954. Enjoying themselves are dancers with organiser PC Len Lea and Mrs Lea (centre).

A Social and reunion was held in March 1954 by members of St Joseph's Catholic Church Matlock when guests included their counterparts from Wirksworth. St Joseph's choir sang and they are pictured performing under their conductor Mr E C Holman at the piano. Left to right are George Phair, Neil Kerr, Walter Kerr, Vincent Hobbs, Anthony Rippon and John Spence. The event was held at the Church Army Social Centre, Matlock Green, where Captain L H Morgan led the square dancing and with his wife served refreshments.

There were a few raised eye-brows when first carpentry and woodworking classes were introduced for women at the Anthony Gell Grammar School. As well as making small tables and stools they learned how to use lathes for making fruit bowls and dishes.

Pictured at the 1951 reunion are members and guests of the Old Wirksworthian Association, including Fred and Chrissie Read, Philip Cash, Mr and Mrs Butlin, Miss Briggs, Mr Young, Mrs Ella Smith, Miss Northrop, Elspeth Gallimore, Joy Coates, Margaret Clay, Beth Bowmer, Geoffrey Kirk, Peter Brewell, Mr Grassby and Mrs Wright.

Wirksworth Congregational Players put on many performances between 1948 and 1962 and in 1951 they produced "The Happiest Days of Your Life" in the Congregational Hall. Left to right (back row) are Jack Craig, John Mitchell, John Dixon, George Guise, Derrick Watts and Geoffrey Kirk; (middle row) Beatrice Antill, Doris Webster, Dorothy Briggs, May Whitehead and Dorothy Mitchell; (front row) Sheila Griffiths and Billy Whitehead.

Brunette Linda Hodgkinson was chosen in April 1954 as the new Well Dressing Queen of Wirksworth. The former head girl of Newbridge School worked at Cooper and Roe's. Appointed as her senior attendants were Alice King and Ann Slack. Judges were Mrs E Finney, Miss Judith O'Connor, Miss Betty Howell and Matlock Councillor Remo Tinti. Also nominated by their respective schools were junior attendants Norma Spencer, Barbara Fearn, Tessa Whitehead and Janet Slack with Alan Brewer and David Slack as pageboys. Chairman of the Well Dressing committee Ken Britland and secretary Frank Gratton are also pictured.

Well dressing festivals are usually held to give blessings for the gift of water, and this year's event at Wirksworth had plenty of it on the the opening day. Queen of the wells was 16-year-old Miss Joan Brooks who was crowned by Mrs John Hadfield, wife of the chairman and managing director of Derbyshire Stone Ltd. Also pictured at the ceremony are Councillor Hubert Doxey, attendants Erica Parsons and Patricia Hopps, maids Vivien Clacker and Ann Field and pages Keith Parsons and Glyn Giles.

Petallers working on the "The Holy Bible" tableau.

Second prize went to Wirksworth Labour and Social Club's "The Holy Bible" designed by Mr W Lowe.

Queen Joy Fearn presents the first prize and trophy to Ken and Mrs Harris, designers of the Wirksworth OAP Association well "I Thirst".

Entrants in the carnival at Wirksworth.

Queens met at Wirksworth in 1955 when 17-year-old Joy Fearn was crowned Queen of the Wells by Mollie McKenzie, Britain's Ballroom Queen. Pictured with them are Linda Hodgkinson (retiring queen), Judith Goodhead, Doreen Thornley, Jean Kinder, Sylvia Buxton, Joy Gratton, Ernestine Jepson, Anne Slack, Alice King, Norma Spencer, Barbara Fearn, Tessa Whitehead, Joy Gratton, Michael Lowe and John Wood.

Winners of the South Peak football league championship at the end of the 1951–52 were Wirksworth Newbridge School. Under the guidance of Headmaster Joe Cresswell and Les Hudson they overcame stiff opposition and here proudly show off their trophy. Left to right (back row) Mr Cresswell, C Slack, D Hodgkinson, C Woodward, F Harrison, D Moxon, V Strilkowski, Mr Hudson; (front row) A Bunting, G Vallance, P Hawley (capt), E Shimwell. D Rowland.

A happy Wirksworth Newbridge School football team poses for the camera in November 1958 after beating Darley Dale Secondary School in a Matlock and District Schools League game that took them to the top of the table. Pictured are Slack, Bark, Morley, Warner, Bowmer, Hallows, Coles, Taylor, Smith, Else (captain) and Spencer with PE and sports master Alan Perry.

The second game at Causeway Lane on Good Friday was the DFA Medals Final when Youlgrave FC trounced Wirksworth Ivanhoe by four goals to nil. A goal by Malcolm White after only ten seconds shook Wirksworth and they never recovered.

Wirksworth Ivanhoe picture includes Michael Hall, John Buckley, Peter Brewell, John Linthwaite, Charles Hallows, David Hallows, Dick Benyon, Ken Britland, Gordon Slack, Peter Haworth, Gerald Bunting, Billy Mather, Derek Moxon and Sam Buckley.

After four seasons as runners-up in the South Peak Senior football league, Wirksworth Newbridge finally became champions in 1953. Pictured with Headmaster Joe Cresswell and games master Les Hudson are J Walker, B Dowson, B Fearn, M Else, D Hurt (captain), R Brownlee, Ken Wilson, J Kirkland, J Seeds, J Ferris, M Shimwell, K Gell and D Morley.

For the second successive year Wirksworth Newbridge School won the South Peak Sports in 1952 held on the Causeway Lane Ground in Matlock. With their sports master Des Marsden and headmaster Joe Cresswell they are Peter Burge, Veronica Shimwell, R Boden, Derek Moxon, M Brewell, Christine Watson, Gerald Vallance, Betty Gilbert, Judy Goodhead, A Watson, Vitali Strilkowski, Roy Hicklin.

Judges and officials at the South Peak Schools Sports in 1952 were Messrs Richard Wragg, Swindell, Rowbottom, Charles Bartram, Bunting, Jack Routledge and Henshaw.

Rivalry between Wirksworth Grammar School and Wirksworth Newbridge School (pictured above) was always keen and no time more so than when they met on Matlock's Causeway Lane ground in the final of the South Peak Schools cricket competition in 1954. Newbridge batted first in the 22-over match and scored 85 for 6 while their opponents could only reply with 42 for 7. Left to right (back row) are J Hayes, G Smith, G Wanford, M Upton, Headmaster J Cresswell, E Holmes, D Morley, G Smith and sports teacher L J Hudson, (front row) F White, B Fearn, B Wanford (captain), F Gell and M Shimwell.

Youlgrave

A local football team to be feared in the Derbyshire Dales during the 50s was Youlgrave – winners of many trophies and medals. One such team to come up against them in 1953 was Wensley, the only undefeated team in the Bakewell and District League at that time. An early injury to a visiting player meant a hastily re-arranged team and up to that point Wensley were holding their own although a goal down scored by Moran. Further goals by Frost and Moran sealed the result and Youlgrave added another scalp to their tally. The Youlgrave team was: left to right (back row) Aaron Taylor (trainer), Cliff Haywood, Len Gladwin, Peter Coleman, Wilf Lincoln (captain), Keith Taylor, Geoff Wragg and Ellis Bowering (linesman); (front row) Arthur Marsden (manager), Jock Moran, Max Dakin, Brian Frost, Rex Bacon, Norman Gladwin, Brian Coleman.

One of the most popular local dancing schools of the 50s was Mrs Swift's of the Northwood School of Dancing. Dozens of stage-struck youngsters attended her classes at the Northwood Club and Youlgrave Village Hall and took part in regular concerts and pantomimes. One such pantomine in 1954 was "Queen of Hearts", performed in Darley Dale Methodist Schoolroom with a cast of nearly 40. Some of those on stage included June Gannicott, Pat Hulley, Pat Mellor, Hilary Birds, Annette Bosley, Vivienne Wragg, Shirley Wagstaffe, Heather Davis, Christine Shimwell, Eileen Fraser, Kathleen Shimwell, Judith Wardman, Veronica Knighton, Hilary Bowler, Aileen Crookes, Jaccqueline Bowler, Jill Wardman, Rona Roose, Christine Bosley, Vivien Tabernor, Barbara Hibbs and Roslyn Roose.

Visitors from far and wide flocked to Youlgrave in 1952 to take part in the annual well dressings opening service. Led by the Rev Dr P Hadfield and the Rev Dr J A Findlay, they were joined by well dressers, Scouts and Cubs, Sunday School scholars and Non-conformist scholars. Youlgrave Band accompanied the singing of the hymns. The Bank Top well (Naboth's Vineyard) was designed by Mr S Shimwell and the Coldwell End well (Born to be King) by Miss M Boardman. The Last Piece of Silver at the Reading Room well was designed by Mr H Lee and the Fountain well (The Prodigal Son) by Mr W Clark.

Attention to detail was the hallmark of Youlgrave well dressings in 1954 and this one depicting Samuel was no exception.

Youlgrave well dressings in 1955 lived up to their usual high standard. Holy Well featured Saul as a boy in Tarsus.

Despite poor weather, Youlgrave well-dressings in 1958 proved to be their usual draw, with visitors arriving from surrounding counties to marvel at the intricate and colourful tableaux. The Bank Top well is pictured designed by Mr Frank Shimwell.

Miss Derbyshire

Buxton girl Sylvia Woodroffe (17) was crowned "Miss Derbyshire 1955" in July at the Grand Pavilion, Matlock Bath. Twelve village and town queens lined up before the judging panel which included Mollie Mackenzie, the National Ballroom Dancing Queen. Sylvia was the second Buxton girl to win the coveted title and trophy – Joan Mellor won in 1950, the year the contest was inaugurated. Runner-up in 1955 was Joyce Minshull (15), of Chapel-en-le-Frith. Other competitors were Barbara Pugh (19, Newbold), Mavis Parker (18, Beeley), Jean Brealey (15, Peak Dale), Brenda Gosney (16, Grindleford), Glenys Gregory (16, Dove Holes), Madeline Plant (15, Whaley Bridge), Shirley Rhodes (17, Starkholmes), Gwen Hadfield (15, Hayfield), Janet Batterley (17, Cromford), and Pamela Toft (20, Duffield). Pictured (left to right) are Janet Batterley, Sylvia Woodroffe, Joyce Minshull and retiring Miss Derbyshire Pat Gannon of Bakewell.

For the fourth consecutive year and fifth overall a Buxton girl won the coveted title of "Miss Derbyshire 1958." She was Miss Maureen Doggett (16) a machinist, and runner-up was Miss Sylvia Orchard (17), a photographic assistant from Derby. Sixteen entrants were judged by Miss Joy Price, Miss E C Harrison and Mr D Neill, and train-bearers were Angela White and her twin sisters Linda and Carol. Pictured are Dorothy Breeze (Ashbourne), Jean Andrew (Bakewell), Rita Hill (Biggin), Wendy Firth (Chapel-en-le-Frith), Jennifer Inckle (Cromford), Norma Elizabeth Ricards (Derby), Jean Burton (Dove Holes), Judith Ann King (Frecheville), Vida Page (Glapwell), Florence Burton (Harpur Hill), Valerie Shaw (Hayfield), Margaret Davey (Spondon), Rosalind Margaret Oldfield (Tideswell), Valerie Betton (Tupton) and Sheila Jarvis (Whaley Bridge).

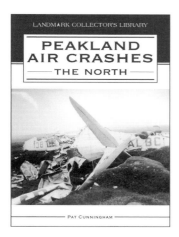

Covers 117 crash sites; includes many illustrations and witness interviews. Volumes 1 & 2 also available on the South and Central areas
ISBN:978-184306-330-8 (13digit)
ISBN:1-84306-330-1
192pp, paperback, £14.99

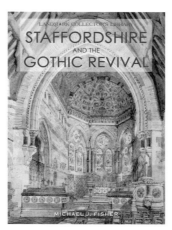

Five architects produced their best ecclesiastical work in Staffordshire.
A tour de force on Victorian Gothic Revival.
ISBN: 978-1-84306-221-9 (13 digit)
ISBN:1-84306-221-6
160pp, paperback, £16.99

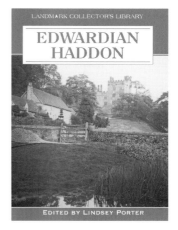

Nearly 50, recently discovered, early photographs, accompany a comprehensive Edwardian description of the finest fortified medieval house in the country.
ISBN: 978-1-84306-320-9 (13 digit)
ISBN:1-84306-320-4
Approx 112pp, paperback, c. £10.99

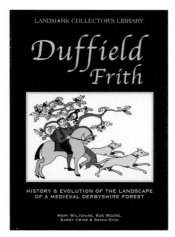

The first comprehensive story of a mid-Derbyshire medieval forest which developed over centuries into a royal forest. Many illustrations.
ISBN: 978-1-84306-191-5 (13 digit)
ISBN:1-84306-191-0
176pp, hardback, £19.99

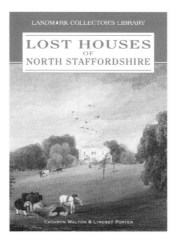

A reminder of nearly 100 former country seats and other houses, many of which no longer survive.
ISBN: 978-1-84306-195-3 (13 digit)
ISBN:1-84306-195-3
160pp, paperback, £14.99

Covers the villages of Beeley, Edensor and Pilsley includes over 300 photographs.
ISBN: 978-1-84306-198-4 (13 digit)
ISBN:1-84306-198-8
144pp, paperback, £14.99

To order please telephone: 01335 347349, Fax: 01335 347303
or email: landmark@clara.net
Landmark Publishing Ltd, Ashbourne Hall, Cokayne Avenue, Ashbourne, Derbyshire DE6 1EJ